D1242915

INSIDE THE
NFL

BALTIMORE
RAVENS

BY WILLIAM MEIER

SportsZone

An Imprint of Abdo Publishing
abdobooks.com

abdobooks.com

Published by Abdo Publishing, a division of ABDO, PO Box 398166, Minneapolis, Minnesota 55439. Copyright © 2020 by Abdo Consulting Group, Inc. International copyrights reserved in all countries. No part of this book may be reproduced in any form without written permission from the publisher. SportsZone™ is a trademark and logo of Abdo Publishing.

Printed in the United States of America, North Mankato, Minnesota
042019
092019

Cover Photo: Gail Burton/AP Images
Interior Photos: Elise Amendola/AP Images, 5; Chuck Burton/AP Images, 7; Rick Bowmer/ AP Images, 11; John Dunn/AP Images, 13; Wally Santana/AP Images, 15; Doug Pensinger/ Getty Images Sport/Getty Images, 16, 43; AP Images, 18; Bill Kostroun/AP Images, 20; Rusty Kennedy/AP Images, 23, 31; Gail Burton/AP Images, 24, 27; G Fiume/Getty Images Sport/Getty Images, 29; Rob Carr/AP Images, 32; Nick Laham/Getty Images Sport/Getty Images, 35; Dilip Vishwanat/Getty Images Sport Classic/Getty Images, 38; Peter G. Aiken/ Getty Images Sport/Getty Images, 40

Editor: Patrick Donnelly
Series Designer: Craig Hinton

Library of Congress Control Number: 2018965353

Publisher's Cataloging-in-Publication Data

Names: Meier, William, author.
Title: Baltimore Ravens / by William Meier
Description: Minneapolis, Minnesota: Abdo Publishing, 2020 | Series: Inside the NFL | Includes
        online resources and index.
Identifiers: ISBN 9781532118388 (lib. bdg.) | ISBN 9781532172564 (ebook)
Subjects: LCSH: Baltimore Ravens (Football team)--Juvenile literature. | National Football
        League--Juvenile literature. | Football teams--Juvenile literature. | American football--
        Juvenile literature.
Classification: DDC 796.33264--dc23

TABLE OF CONTENTS

CHAPTER 1

GREATEST DEFENSE EVER?

Which National Football League (NFL) team had the best defense of all time? It's a question that football fans have debated for years. Legendary teams are mentioned often when the topic comes up. One of them is the 2000 Baltimore Ravens.

In 2000 the Ravens featured a rugged, swarming defense that led the team all the way to a Super Bowl title. In the regular season, Baltimore set NFL records for fewest points (165) and rushing yards (970) allowed in a 16-game schedule. The Ravens shut out four opponents. They did not have the most talented offense. But on the strength of that amazing defense, Baltimore finished 12–4 and earned a wild-card playoff spot.

Duane Starks (top) and Chris McAlister celebrate Starks's touchdown in the Super Bowl.

THE "D" DEBATE

What are some of the other greatest defenses in NFL history? The 1985 Chicago Bears, led by standouts such as linebacker Mike Singletary and defensive end Richard Dent, went 15–1 and won a Super Bowl crown with a tough-as-nails defense.

In the 1970s, the Pittsburgh Steelers defense was known as the "Steel Curtain." It included Hall of Fame players such as defensive tackle "Mean" Joe Greene. Four Steelers teams from the 1970s won Super Bowls. In the 1970s, the Minnesota Vikings' "Purple People Eaters" defense featured multiple Hall of Famers. The 1986 and 1990 New York Giants won Super Bowls with the help of stout defenses. Hall of Fame linebacker Lawrence Taylor was their star.

In the postseason, the defense played even better. Baltimore was stingy in allowing other teams to score. In the first two rounds, the Ravens defeated the visiting Denver Broncos 21–3 and the host Tennessee Titans 24–10.

Then in the American Football Conference (AFC) Championship Game at Oakland, the Ravens forced five Raiders turnovers. Baltimore also held Oakland to 24 rushing yards on 17 carries in a 16–3 victory. A 96-yard touchdown pass in the second quarter from Trent Dilfer to tight end Shannon Sharpe was all the offense the Ravens needed that day.

Linebacker Ray Lewis, shown during a playoff game against the Titans in January 2001, was the leader of the Ravens' superb defense.

"We've got one more challenge," Baltimore defensive coordinator Marvin Lewis said of his defense afterward, referring to the Super Bowl. "They want to make their mark in history."

BRIAN BILLICK

The head coach of the 2000 Ravens was Brian Billick. He was hired before the 1999 season. He had been the offensive coordinator for the Minnesota Vikings from 1993 to 1998. In 1998 the Vikings scored a record 556 points under Billick's guidance. With the Ravens, he found himself in charge of a team known for its dominant defense. Billick proved that he could change his coaching style. The Vikings had thrown the ball often under Billick. But the Ravens' offense tried to use up time on the clock by running frequently. This kept the defenders well rested, allowing them to dominate when they were on the field.

Ray Lewis, who was named the 2000 NFL Defensive Player of the Year, led the Ravens' defense. Peter Boulware and Jamie Sharper formed a standout linebacker trio with Lewis. Sam Adams and Tony Siragusa were excellent run stoppers at the tackle positions. Ends Rob Burnett and Michael McCrary pressured the quarterback. The secondary, led by future Hall of Famer Rod Woodson at safety and cornerbacks Chris McAlister and Duane Starks, shut down opponents' passing attacks.

Baltimore's offense was not flashy. But it played well enough to help the team win. The veteran Dilfer replaced Tony Banks as the starting quarterback partway through the season and finished with 12 touchdown passes against 11 interceptions. Rookie running back Jamal Lewis rushed for 1,364 yards. Sharpe was the team's top pass catcher with 67 receptions. On special teams, the Ravens had standout players in speedy return man Jermaine Lewis and reliable kicker Matt Stover.

But the 2000 Ravens were known for their defense. The defense demonstrated to the world just how good it was when Baltimore faced the New York Giants in Super Bowl XXXV on January 28, 2001, in Tampa, Florida.

The game turned into a showcase for the Ravens' defense. Baltimore allowed just 152 yards, forced five turnovers, recorded four sacks, and did not give up an offensive touchdown in a 34–7 win. The Ravens forced the Giants' Kerry Collins into 15-for-39 passing for just 112 yards.

Dilfer's 38-yard touchdown pass to Brandon Stokley in the first quarter and Stover's 47-yard field goal in the second staked the Ravens to a 10–0 lead at halftime. In the third quarter, Starks intercepted a Collins pass and returned it 49 yards for a touchdown, giving the Ravens a 17–0 lead.

The only blemish for Baltimore came when Ron Dixon's 97-yard kickoff return for a touchdown cut the Ravens' lead to 17–7. But Baltimore responded to that immediately with Jermaine Lewis's 84-yard kickoff return for a touchdown that put Baltimore ahead 24–7. In the fourth quarter, Jamal Lewis ran for a 3-yard touchdown and Stover made a 34-yard

Trent Dilfer was the Ravens' starting quarterback for much of their championship run in 2000. Dilfer had played his first six NFL seasons with Tampa Bay. The Buccaneers released him in February 2000. The Ravens signed him the next month to serve as the backup quarterback to Tony Banks. Banks struggled early in the 2000 season, and Dilfer took over as the starter. The Ravens lost the first game that he started but won the final 11, counting the playoffs. After the 2000 season, Dilfer signed with the Seattle Seahawks. He only spent one year in Baltimore, but it was a huge success.

field goal. The Giants gained just one first down on their final four possessions.

Dilfer threw no interceptions. Jamal Lewis ran for 102 yards on 27 carries. Again, the Ravens got the job done with an efficient performance from the offense and a dominant effort from the defense.

Ray Lewis was named the Super Bowl Most Valuable Player (MVP). The heart and soul of the Ravens' defense finished with 11 tackles and six assists.

"Our defense has been doing this all year," the linebacker said. "No one can ever take this away from us. We're the best ever."

On January 30, 2001, the Ravens held a victory parade through downtown Baltimore. Rain and cold weather did not stop more than 200,000 people from packing the streets and celebrating the team's Super Bowl title.

✖ Super Bowl MVP Ray Lewis smiles after the Ravens routed the Giants.

The 2000 season was a magical ride for the Ravens. Making it even more special for fans in Baltimore was that the team was in just its fifth season of existence. Baltimore was no stranger to the NFL, though. The city had been home to an NFL team before—the Baltimore Colts—only to see it leave. With the Ravens, "Charm City," as Baltimore is known, was thrilled to have a championship franchise again.

CHAPTER 2

BALTIMORE'S SECOND CHANCE

Long before the Ravens ever played in Baltimore, the Maryland city had another NFL team. The Colts played in Baltimore from 1953 through 1983 and won four NFL titles, the most recent after the 1970 season.

But in March 1984, the Colts' owner decided to move the team to Indianapolis. Baltimore fans were crushed. But they never stopped hoping for a new team.

Their chance came in 1995. Cleveland Browns owner Art Modell was not happy with the condition of his team's aging stadium. Late that year, Modell announced that he was moving the tradition-rich Browns from Cleveland to Baltimore, where a new stadium would be built.

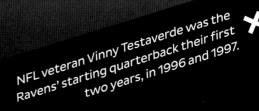

NFL veteran Vinny Testaverde was the Ravens' starting quarterback their first two years, in 1996 and 1997.

The city of Cleveland tried to prevent the Browns from leaving. Eventually, a settlement was reached in which Cleveland would get an NFL expansion team in 1999. That team would be called the Browns and be considered the same franchise as the old Browns franchise. The team that moved to Baltimore in 1996 would get a different name and be thought of as a new franchise. But it would inherit the Browns' players.

The Baltimore team needed a name. The franchise had the *Baltimore Sun* newspaper conduct a poll. The three nickname finalists were Ravens, Americans, and Marauders. Ravens received the most votes by far. On March 29, 1996, the team was officially named the Ravens. The name honored Edgar Allan Poe, who penned his famous poem "The Raven" while living in Baltimore. The Ravens chose purple, black, gold, and white as their team colors.

The next step was the team's first NFL Draft on April 20. With their first two picks, the Ravens chose offensive tackle Jonathan Ogden (fourth overall) and linebacker Ray Lewis (twenty-sixth overall). Both would become Hall of Famers.

The Browns had struggled in the seasons before the team moved to Baltimore in 1996. It would take time for the Ravens to build a winner. Still, fans in Baltimore were pumped up for

NFL Commissioner Paul Tagliabue introduces Jonathan Ogden as the Ravens' first-ever draft pick in 1996.

the 1996 season opener on September 1 at Memorial Stadium. It was the same stadium that the Baltimore Colts had played in. The Ravens would need to play at Memorial Stadium until a new stadium was ready.

× Running back Earnest Byner fights for yardage against the Raiders in the Ravens' first regular-season game.

The Ravens won that first game, beating the Oakland Raiders 19–14 in front of 64,124 fans. Quarterback Vinny Testaverde scored the game's first touchdown on a 9-yard run. Matt Stover made two field goals. Earnest Byner's 1-yard touchdown run in the fourth quarter was the decisive score.

VINNY TESTAVERDE

Vinny Testaverde had already played nine seasons in the NFL when the Ravens made their debut in 1996. Testaverde won the Heisman Trophy in 1986 while playing at the University of Miami. Tampa Bay selected him with the first pick in the 1987 NFL Draft. He mostly struggled during six seasons with the Buccaneers. He then signed with Cleveland and improved. Testaverde made the move with the Browns to Baltimore in 1996. He excelled during the Ravens' first year, enjoying one of his finest seasons in the NFL with 4,177 passing yards and 33 touchdown passes. He would play one more season with the Ravens and then sign with the New York Jets. Testaverde continued to play in the NFL through 2007, when he retired at age 44.

The rest of the season would not go as well for the Ravens. The team was competitive in many games but went 4–12. Baltimore finished in last place in the AFC Central Division.

Testaverde's play was a pleasant surprise in 1996. The veteran had his best season in the NFL to that point. Wide receivers Michael Jackson (76 catches for 1,201 yards) and Derrick Alexander (62 catches for 1,099 yards) were key factors in the passing attack. The team's defense struggled, however.

The Ravens got off to a solid start in 1997, winning three of their first four games. But they went 1–7–1 in their next nine.

Fans arrive at the new Ravens Stadium for Baltimore's first game there, an exhibition contest in August 1998 against the Chicago Bears.

The Ravens finished 6–9–1 and again found themselves in last place in the AFC Central.

But the team's defense was starting to come together. Rookie linebacker Peter Boulware finished with 11.5 sacks and was selected as the NFL Defensive Rookie of the Year. Ray Lewis was also sensational with a league-leading 184 tackles. He was selected to his first Pro Bowl.

Baltimore finished 1998 with a 6–10 record and in fourth place. The Ravens had trouble on offense that season. The defense added a key player when future Hall of Fame defensive back Rod Woodson signed with the team before the season began. After spending 10 years with the Pittsburgh Steelers, Woodson had played one year for the San Francisco 49ers before he signed with Baltimore.

The Ravens decided not to renew coach Ted Marchibroda's contract after the 1998 season. They hired former Minnesota offensive coordinator Brian Billick as his replacement. Billick had helped guide the Vikings' record-setting offense in 1998.

Baltimore got off to another slow start in 1999, losing five of its first seven games. Then the team got hot toward the end of the season. The Ravens were 8–7 going

NO PLACE LIKE HOME

On September 6, 1998, the Ravens opened the season with a game against the Pittsburgh Steelers. The contest was the first at the Ravens' sparkling new stadium, then called Ravens Stadium at Camden Yards.

Ground was broken for the football-only facility in mid-1996. The stadium was built downtown, adjacent to Oriole Park at Camden Yards—the home of the Baltimore Orioles baseball team. Ravens Stadium was constructed to seat approximately 70,000 people. It cost an estimated $220 million and was paid for by a combination of public and team funds.

× Rod Woodson returns an interception in 1998. The defensive back was a key part of the Ravens' defense from 1998 to 2001.

into the final week. They had a chance to make the playoffs but lost 20–3 to the New England Patriots.

Baltimore saw improvement on offense in 1999. But the most noticeable change was that the Ravens defense had improved dramatically. Baltimore ranked sixth in the NFL in points allowed and second in yards allowed. It was led by Ray Lewis (168 tackles, three interceptions), Woodson (seven interceptions), and Boulware (10 sacks). Rookie Chris McAlister was an immediate standout with five interceptions, while defensive end Michael McCrary's 11.5 sacks were the most by any Raven.

The Ravens' success at the end of 1999 carried over into the 2000 season. The defense got even better. It all added up to a Super Bowl title and the most memorable season in team history.

SHANNON SHARPE

Tight end Shannon Sharpe played only two seasons with the Ravens. But they were extremely memorable. Sharpe came to Baltimore in 2000 after 10 seasons in Denver. His 96-yard touchdown catch in the AFC Championship Game helped Baltimore reach its first Super Bowl. It was the longest touchdown catch ever in a playoff game. In 2001 Sharpe passed Browns legend Ozzie Newsome for most catches and receiving yards by a tight end. He also made the Pro Bowl. Sharpe returned to Denver for two more seasons, then retired after 2003. He was inducted into the Pro Football Hall of Fame in 2011.

Living up to the 2000 season was perhaps an impossible task. The Ravens would be reminded of that repeatedly over the rest of the decade. But the defense, led by Lewis, would continue to impress.

CHAPTER 3

TRYING TO RECAPTURE GLORY

Trent Dilfer did not get to enjoy his Super Bowl win in Baltimore. The Ravens released him before the 2001 season. It was an unpopular decision among players and fans. The team signed Pro Bowl quarterback Elvis Grbac from the Chiefs instead.

The 2001 Ravens' attempt to defend their title took a huge blow before the season even started. Jamal Lewis suffered a season-ending knee injury in training camp. Despite this, Baltimore finished 10–6 and sneaked into the playoffs as a wild card. Baltimore beat the host Miami Dolphins 20–3 in the first round but then fell 27–10 at Pittsburgh in the divisional round. Grbac threw three

Elvis Grbac (18) had a rough go of it during his only season as the Ravens' starting quarterback.

Ravens owner Art Modell, *left*, and general manager Ozzie Newsome, *right*, pose with 2003 draft picks Kyle Boller and Terrell Suggs.

interceptions against the Steelers. He was released after the season and ended up retiring from the NFL.

In 2002 Baltimore lost several key players from the Super Bowl team. The lack of experience and mediocre quarterback play from journeyman Jeff Blake led to a 7–9 season. The Ravens began the 2003 season with yet another new quarterback—rookie Kyle Boller. Baltimore selected Boller with the nineteenth pick in the NFL Draft. The team also drafted linebacker Terrell Suggs with the tenth overall choice.

Boller started nine games in 2003. Baltimore finished 5–4 in them. When Boller went down with a season-ending thigh injury in November, backup Anthony Wright stepped up and led the team to five victories in its final six games. The Ravens finished 10–6 and won the AFC North title. It was the first division championship in team history.

The defense was key to Baltimore's success in 2003. Suggs finished with 12 sacks and was named the NFL Defensive Rookie of the Year. Of course, the Ravens still had star linebacker Ray Lewis. He finished with 161 tackles and six interceptions. He was chosen as the NFL Defensive Player of the Year for the second time. Second-year safety Ed Reed intercepted seven passes and was selected to the first of his nine career Pro Bowls.

Running back Jamal Lewis also played a huge role for the Ravens

JONATHAN OGDEN

Through the Ravens' ups and downs, offensive tackle Jonathan Ogden was consistently excellent. Baltimore selected Ogden, a former standout at the University of California, Los Angeles (UCLA), with the first draft choice in team history, fourth overall in 1996. Ogden made his first Pro Bowl after the 1997 season, his second year in the NFL. He would make the Pro Bowl every season through 2007 and be chosen as an All-Pro nine times. The 6-foot-9, 340-pound Ogden excelled at pass blocking and run blocking. Ogden retired after the 2007 season and was inducted into the Hall of Fame in 2013.

ED REED

The Ravens chose safety Ed Reed with the No. 24 pick in the 2002 NFL Draft. Like linebacker Ray Lewis, Reed had played at the University of Miami in Florida. Also like Lewis, Reed would become one of the top defensive players in the NFL.

Reed was selected as the NFL Defensive Player of the Year in 2004. He made nine Pro Bowls and had 64 career interceptions. Reed played in Baltimore until 2012, then played one more season, half with Houston and half with the New York Jets, before retiring. He was inducted into the Pro Football Hall of Fame in 2019.

Reed broke his own league record when he returned an interception 107 yards for a touchdown in 2008. He intercepted the ball deep in the end zone and returned it all the way to the other end zone against the Philadelphia Eagles on November 23. His previous record was 106 yards. Reed finished his career with the most interception return yards in NFL history.

in 2003. Lewis rushed for 2,066 yards—second-most in NFL history at the time—and 14 touchdowns. He also set an NFL single-game record with 295 rushing yards in Baltimore's 33–13 home win over Cleveland in the second week. Third-year tight end Todd Heap had 57 catches, leading the team in receptions for the second straight year.

The Ravens played host to the Tennessee Titans in the first round of the playoffs on January 3, 2004. But Titans kicker

Ravens safety Ed Reed (20) developed a knack for making big plays in the secondary and on special teams.

Gary Anderson made a 46-yard field goal with 29 seconds remaining to lift Tennessee to a 20–17 victory. Jamal Lewis was held to 35 rushing yards.

The Ravens stumbled to a 9–7 record in 2004. A lone bright spot was Reed winning NFL Defensive Player of the Year. Injuries to him, Ray Lewis, and Boller led to a 6–10 record in 2005. Baltimore would change direction again at quarterback before the 2006 season. It would turn out to be the Ravens' best move at that position since signing Dilfer.

CHAPTER 4

RETURN TO WINNING WAYS

The Ravens' defense had remained strong in the seasons after the 2000 team's Super Bowl triumph. The problem was that the offense did not play well. In particular, the quarterback position was a concern.

In June 2006, Baltimore found the quarterback it was seeking. The Ravens traded a fourth-round draft pick to the Tennessee Titans for veteran Steve McNair. McNair was a tough player. He would show that toughness with Baltimore in 2006, his twelfth season in the NFL.

McNair stepped in as the starting quarterback. Kyle Boller was his backup. The Ravens had improved their receiving corps before the previous season when they signed Derrick Mason, a former teammate of McNair's in Tennessee.

Quarterback Steve McNair had a strong 2006 season in Baltimore.

They had also drafted wide receiver Mark Clayton in the first round out of the University of Oklahoma. Mason, Clayton, and tight end Todd Heap formed a solid pass-catching trio.

MATT STOVER

Kicker Matt Stover played for the Ravens from their first season, 1996, through 2008. Stover was a Cleveland Brown from 1991 to 1995, then moved with the team when it relocated to Baltimore in 1996. In 2006 he made 28 of 30 field-goal tries for an accuracy of 93.3 percent, the best in the NFL that season. The Ravens decided not to sign Stover before the 2009 season. Stover, in turn, signed with Indianapolis. On February 7, 2010, he became the oldest player to participate in a Super Bowl, at the age of 42 years, 11 days. He made a 38-yard field goal in the Colts' 31–17 loss to the New Orleans Saints.

Baltimore's stronger passing attack, combined with the running of a healthy Jamal Lewis and a still-ferocious defense, was a winning formula in 2006. McNair started all 16 games. He finished with 16 touchdown passes against 12 interceptions. Heap (73 catches), Mason (68), and Clayton (67) were McNair's favorite targets. Lewis rushed for 1,132 yards and nine touchdowns. Baltimore's defense ranked first in the NFL in yards and points allowed. It all added up to a 13–3 record and an AFC North title.

The Ravens received a bye in the first round of the playoffs. In the next round, they hosted the Indianapolis Colts in a battle of the two NFL teams to call Baltimore

Colts defensive tackle Raheem Brock (79) stuffs Ravens running back Jamal Lewis in Indianapolis' 15–6 playoff win on January 13, 2007.

their home. Indianapolis was no pushover. The team went 12–4 in the regular season and had a star in Peyton Manning, who drew comparisons to another legendary quarterback in Colts history—Johnny Unitas.

Ravens owner Steve Bisciotti, *left*, and coach John Harbaugh appear at a news conference after Harbaugh was hired in January 2008.

It was Indianapolis' defense, though, not Manning, that led the team to victory. Adam Vinatieri kicked five field goals, and the Colts kept the Ravens out of the end zone in a 15–6 win. Baltimore committed four turnovers.

Injuries derailed the Ravens' 2007 campaign. McNair played in just six games. Baltimore finished 5–11. Owner Steve Bisciotti fired head coach Brian Billick the day after the season ended.

McNair and standout offensive tackle Jonathan Ogden announced their retirements after the 2007 season. Bisciotti, meanwhile, hired John Harbaugh to be the third coach in Ravens history. Harbaugh was a longtime special teams coordinator with the Philadelphia Eagles.

The Ravens used their first draft choice in 2008, the eighteenth pick overall, on quarterback Joe Flacco. Some questioned whether Flacco, who played at the University of Delaware, could make a successful jump to the NFL. Delaware did not compete against the top level of competition in the college ranks. Flacco got the chance right away to show if he belonged among the NFL's elite quarterbacks.

JOHN HARBAUGH

Ravens coach John Harbaugh comes from a football family. His father, Jack, was a high school and college coach for 41 years. John's brother Jim played quarterback for 14 seasons in the NFL, including in 1998 with the Ravens, and then got into coaching. He coached the San Francisco 49ers before leaving to coach the University of Michigan. John had been a college assistant before the Philadelphia Eagles hired him in 1998. He served as the special teams coordinator and then defensive backs coach for the Eagles.

CHAPTER 5

SUPER AGAIN

A new era for the Ravens began in 2008. Rookie coach John Harbaugh and rookie quarterback Joe Flacco both made impressive debuts in their new positions. Baltimore finished 11–5, one game behind Pittsburgh in the AFC North. The Ravens earned a wild-card playoff berth.

In the first round of the AFC playoffs, the Ravens routed the Dolphins 27–9 in Miami. Ed Reed had two interceptions, returning one of them 64 yards for a touchdown. In the next round, Baltimore edged host Tennessee 13–10.

The Ravens advanced to the AFC Championship Game to face the Steelers in Pittsburgh. The game was physical. Flacco was sacked three times and threw three interceptions. Pittsburgh won 23–14 and went on to win the Super Bowl.

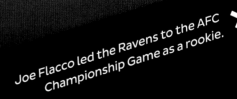

Joe Flacco led the Ravens to the AFC Championship Game as a rookie.

THE RAY RICE INCIDENT

In Ray Rice, the Ravens thought they had their franchise running back. In his first six seasons, he posted 6,180 rushing yards and 3,034 receiving yards. But before the 2014 season started, Rice was arrested for assaulting his wife. The NFL suspended him for two games. After video of the assault surfaced, the Ravens released Rice. He never played in the NFL again.

Baltimore carried over its success from 2008 into 2009. Flacco continued to play with a maturity beyond his years. Second-year running back Ray Rice emerged as a star. He rushed for 1,339 yards and caught 78 passes. Derrick Mason had another 1,000-yard season. Baltimore's defense remained a strength.

The Ravens finished 9–7 in 2009 and earned another wild-card playoff spot. Baltimore traveled to New England in the postseason's first round. Rice ran for 159 yards and two touchdowns as the Ravens rolled to a 33–14 win. Baltimore intercepted Patriots star quarterback Tom Brady three times.

However, the Ravens' season ended the next week with a 20–3 loss at Indianapolis. The loss was further evidence of a frustrating pattern for Baltimore fans. The Ravens were one of the best teams in the AFC. They regularly got to the playoffs. But they could not beat the conference's top contenders and reach the Super Bowl.

The Steelers knocked the Ravens out again after the 2010 season. Baltimore looked to bounce back in 2011. Terrell Suggs was NFL Defensive Player of the Year, and the team went 12–4. The Ravens won the AFC North for the third time in history.

After beating the Houston Texans in the first round, the Ravens visited the mighty Patriots in the AFC Championship Game. New England was favored by a touchdown, but it was the Ravens who held a 20–16 lead in the fourth quarter.

Brady led a touchdown drive to retake the lead. Baltimore had one last chance to win or tie. Flacco drove the offense to the New England 14-yard line. But a potential game-winning touchdown pass slipped through the hands of wide receiver Lee Evans. Ravens kicker Billy Cundiff came on to try to tie the game. But his 32-yard field-goal attempt hooked wide left, giving the Patriots the Super Bowl berth.

The loss was heartbreaking. It was so hard that Reed considered retirement. But he decided to come back and take another shot at a championship.

"We're a totally different team this year," Reed said the next fall. "We don't even have some of the same guys on the team. It's always a new year the next year."

Ray Lewis, *left*, and Terrell Suggs were a formidable defensive duo for the Ravens.

It was indeed a new Ravens team. But it kept winning with strong defense, led by Reed and Ray Lewis, who at age 37 announced 2012 would be his last season. Flacco turned in a solid year with 22 touchdowns and just 10 interceptions.

Though they won two fewer games, the Ravens won the AFC North again. They crushed the Colts in the first round 24–9. Then they had to go to Denver to face Peyton Manning and the Broncos the second round.

The game was tied at the end of each of the first three quarters. But Denver took a late 35–28 lead. Flacco rescued the Ravens with a 70-yard touchdown pass to Jacoby Jones with 31 seconds left. The game went into overtime.

Then the defense made a huge play. Ravens cornerback Corey Graham intercepted a Manning pass and returned it to the Denver 45-yard line. Six plays later, Justin Tucker's 47-yard field goal won the game for Baltimore.

The AFC Championship Game was a rematch with the Patriots. Trailing 13–7 at halftime, Flacco threw three touchdown passes in the second half, and Baltimore's defense held New England scoreless the rest of the way for a 28–13 win. Finally, Baltimore was going back to the Super Bowl.

Flacco continued his great play in Super Bowl XLVII. He threw three touchdown passes as the Ravens built a 28–6 lead over the San Francisco 49ers. Just as it looked like Baltimore would coast to a title, the lights went out. For real. The lights at the Louisiana Superdome went dark in the third quarter.

After a delay, the 49ers came out playing like a different team. They closed the gap to 34–29 in the fourth quarter and had a chance to take the lead in the game's final moments.

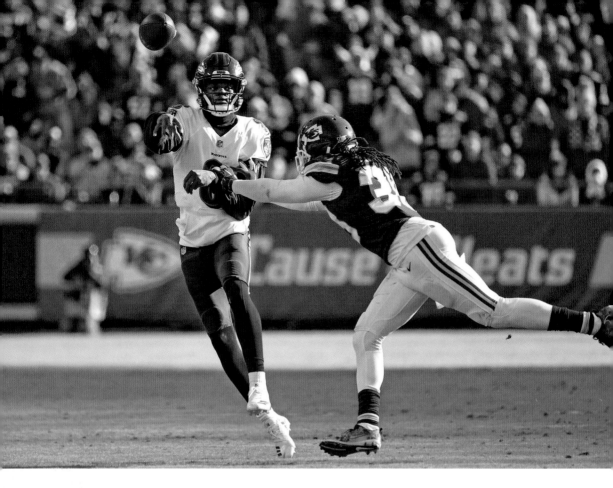

Quarterback Lamar Jackson throws on the run in a 2018 game against the Kansas City Chiefs.

But the Baltimore defense finally got the stop it needed. Niners quarterback Colin Kaepernick came up empty on three straight passes from the Baltimore 5-yard line, and the Ravens held on to win. It was a fitting end to Ray Lewis's career. And Flacco was named the game's MVP.

The Ravens struggled to regain their footing over the next five seasons. They went to the playoffs just once in that span, after the 2014 season. In 2015 they went 5–11, their first losing season since the year before Flacco arrived.

The Ravens began to look to the future in 2018, drafting University of Louisville quarterback Lamar Jackson in the first round. When Flacco suffered a hip injury during a Week 9 loss to the Steelers, Harbaugh handed Jackson the keys to the offense. The rookie rushed for 119 yards in his first start, a 24–21 win over Cincinnati. He had success through the air, too, passing for six touchdowns and just three interceptions as the Ravens won six of their last seven games, all with Jackson under center.

The rookie's strong finish helped the Ravens to another AFC North title. But in his first playoff start, Jackson appeared flustered. He threw an interception and fumbled three times against the Los Angeles Chargers. Though Flacco was available to play, Harbaugh stuck with his young quarterback. However, by the time Jackson recovered to throw two touchdown passes in the fourth quarter, it was too little, too late. The Chargers pulled off a 23–17 upset.

Flacco was traded to the Broncos for a draft pick before the 2019 season. In passing the torch to Jackson, the Ravens hoped they had found their third Super Bowl quarterback.

TIMELINE

The Ravens rally to beat the Indianapolis Colts 38–31 on November 29, marking the old franchise's first game in Baltimore since 1983.

The Ravens lose to the Steelers 20–13 on September 6 in their first game in their new downtown stadium.

On September 1, the Ravens play their first NFL game, defeating the Oakland Raiders 19–14.

The new Baltimore team's name is officially chosen as Ravens on March 29.

On February 9, the NFL approves the relocation of the Cleveland Browns franchise to Baltimore.

1996   **1996**   **1996**   **1998**   **1998**

After a team-best 13–3 regular season, the Ravens fall 15–6 to the visiting Colts on January 13 in the divisional round of the playoffs.

Ravens running back Jamal Lewis sets an NFL single-game record with 295 rushing yards against Cleveland on September 14.

The Ravens crush the New York Giants 34–7 in Super Bowl XXXV on January 28.

The Ravens defeat host Oakland 16–3 in the AFC Championship Game on January 14.

On January 19, former Minnesota Vikings offensive coordinator Brian Billick is named the Ravens' second head coach.

1999   **2001**   **2001**   **2003**   **2007**

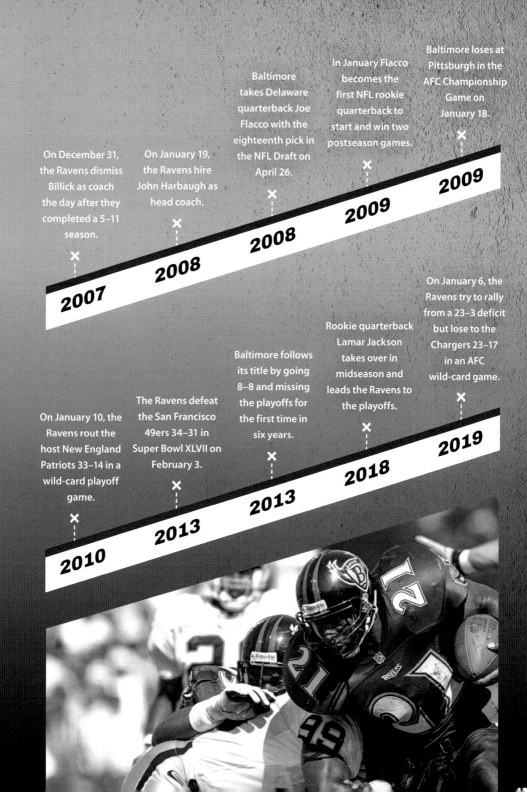

On December 31, the Ravens dismiss Billick as coach the day after they completed a 5–11 season.

❌

2007

On January 19, the Ravens hire John Harbaugh as head coach.

❌

2008

Baltimore takes Delaware quarterback Joe Flacco with the eighteenth pick in the NFL Draft on April 26.

❌

2008

In January Flacco becomes the first NFL rookie quarterback to start and win two postseason games.

❌

2009

Baltimore loses at Pittsburgh in the AFC Championship Game on January 18.

❌

2009

On January 10, the Ravens rout the host New England Patriots 33–14 in a wild-card playoff game.

❌

2010

The Ravens defeat the San Francisco 49ers 34–31 in Super Bowl XLVII on February 3.

❌

2013

Baltimore follows its title by going 8–8 and missing the playoffs for the first time in six years.

❌

2013

Rookie quarterback Lamar Jackson takes over in midseason and leads the Ravens to the playoffs.

❌

2018

On January 6, the Ravens try to rally from a 23–3 deficit but lose to the Chargers 23–17 in an AFC wild-card game.

❌

2019

QUICK STATS

FRANCHISE HISTORY

1996–

SUPER BOWLS
(wins in bold)

2000 (XXXV), **2012** (XLVII)

AFC CHAMPIONSHIP GAMES

2000, 2008, 2011, 2012

DIVISION CHAMPIONSHIPS

2003, 2006, 2011, 2012, 2018

KEY COACHES

Brian Billick (1999–2007): 80–64,
   5–3 (playoffs)
John Harbaugh (2007–):
   104–72, 10–6 (playoffs)

KEY PLAYERS
(position, seasons with team)

Peter Boulware (LB, 1997–2005)
Joe Flacco (QB, 2008–18)
Todd Heap (TE, 2001–10)
Jamal Lewis (RB, 2000, 2002–06)
Ray Lewis (LB, 1996–12)
Chris McAlister (CB, 1999–2008)
Steve McNair (QB, 2006–07)
C. J. Mosley (LB, 2014–18)
Jonathan Ogden (OT, 1996–2007)
Ed Reed (S, 2002–12)
Matt Stover (K, 1996–2008)
Terrell Suggs (LB, 2003–18)
Rod Woodson (DB, 1998–2001)

HOME FIELDS

M&T Bank Stadium (1998–)
   Also known as Ravens Stadium,
   PSINet Stadium
Memorial Stadium (1996–97)

* All statistics through 2018 season

QUOTES AND ANECDOTES

"I've got no problem playing second fiddle to our defense. We do things that make us better. We were second in the league in time of possession. We have a ton of explosive plays. We were best in the league in turnover ratio. My teammates carried me. I don't know how good I am, but I'm the best quarterback for this team right now."

—Quarterback Trent Dilfer, talking during the 2000 playoffs about the offense's contributions to the defense-oriented Ravens' success that season

When the Ravens won Super Bowl XXXV in January 2001, they became the third team in NFL history to win a Super Bowl after making the playoffs as a wild-card team. The 1980 Oakland Raiders and 1997 Denver Broncos also accomplished the feat.

Ravens star safety Ed Reed, who was also a standout on special teams, became the first player in NFL history to score a touchdown on an interception return, a blocked punt, a punt return, and a fumble return. He scored 13 touchdowns in his career—seven on interceptions, three on blocked punts, two on fumble returns, and one on a punt return.

The Baltimore Colts may have left the city in 1984. But their marching band never went anywhere. The former Colts marching band stayed together and performed at other events, including to promote bringing a new team to Baltimore. They performed for two Ravens seasons as the Colts band, then became the Marching Ravens in 1998. The Ravens are one of two teams in the NFL to have their own marching band.

"Every decision is based on what makes us the strongest possible team we can be. . . . That's what it boils down to. That's how we feel about this decision and we're rolling."

—John Harbaugh explaining why he chose Lamar Jackson over Joe Flacco when Flacco returned from injury in December 2018

GLOSSARY

contract
An agreement to play for a certain team.

draft
A system that allows teams to acquire new players coming into a league.

franchise
A sports organization, including the top-level team and all minor league affiliates.

Hall of Fame
The highest honor a player or coach can get when his or her career is over.

legendary
A player who is generally regarded as one of the best to ever play.

postseason
Another word for playoffs; the time after the end of the regular season when teams play to determine a champion.

Pro Bowl
The NFL's all-star game, in which the best players in the league compete.

rookie
A professional athlete in his or her first year of competition.

sack
A tackle of the quarterback behind the line of scrimmage before he can pass the ball.

turnover
Loss of the ball to the other team through an interception or fumble.

MORE INFORMATION

BOOKS

Gitlin, Marty. *Joe Flacco*. Minneapolis, MN: Abdo Publishing, 2014.

Graves, Will. *The Best NFL Defenses of All Time*. Minneapolis, MN: Abdo Publishing, 2013.

Smolka, Bo. *Baltimore Ravens*. Minneapolis, MN: Abdo Publishing, 2017.

ONLINE RESOURCES

Booklinks
NONFICTION NETWORK
FREE! ONLINE NONFICTION RESOURCES

To learn more about the Baltimore Ravens, visit **abdobooklinks.com** or scan this QR code. These links are routinely monitored and updated to provide the most current information available.

PLACE TO VISIT

Ravens Under Armour Performance Center
1 Winning Dr.
Owings Mills, MD 21117
410–701–4000
baltimoreravens.com

The UAPC is the Ravens headquarters as well as home to the team's annual training camp before the start of each season.

INDEX

ABOUT THE AUTHOR

William Meier has worked as an author and editor in the publishing industry for more than 25 years. He resides in St. Louis, Missouri, with his wife and their poodle, Macy.